DISCARDED

R 031 j
R

Disney's
WORLD
OF DISCOVERY

WORLD
OF DISCOVERY
VOLUME 3
Crime–France

GROLIER
INCORPORATED
DANBURY, CONN.

GROLIER INCORPORATED

Robert B. Clarke   Publisher

ISBN: 0-7172-8165-5

Copyright © 1981 by Walt Disney Productions

Library of Congress Catalog Card Number: 81-80044

The material contained herein was previously published under the title Disney's My First Encyclopedia.

PRINTED IN THE UNITED STATES OF AMERICA

What are the symbols for?

Each entry in these books is marked by a symbol. The symbols are a learning aid. They are like road signs. They tell you what direction you are taking as you begin to read about a subject word. If you are looking up python, for example, the symbol tells you that the python is a reptile, one of a group of animals that includes lizards, turtles, and snakes. In this way, the symbols will help you to sort out and organize in your own mind the information you will find in these books.

Amphibians

Ancient History

Animal Behavior

Art and Literature

Birds

Communications

Dinosaurs

Economics

Entertainment

Famous People

Fish

Flowers and Plants

Human Behavior

Human Body

Insects

Mammals

Modern History

Music

Outer Space

Planet Earth

Pond and Ocean Life

Religions

Reptiles

Science

Sports

Transportation

Trees

World Affairs

Crime

Crime is a threat to society. Policemen and women use wanted posters (a), laboratory research (b), handcuffs (c), fingerprints (d), whistles (e), nightsticks (f), and guns (g) to fight crime.

A person who breaks a law commits a crime. Some crimes are more serious than others. A serious crime, like robbery or kidnapping, is called a felony. Less serious crimes, such as traffic violations, are called misdemeanors.

A person who commits a crime is called a criminal. A criminal may commit a crime against people, such as murder. Or a criminal may commit a crime against property, such as burning down a building or stealing.

There have been crimes ever since people first began to live together. Over the years, laws have been passed that made certain acts a crime. These laws also list the punishment for the crime. The purpose of these laws is to protect society against criminals. Criminals are sent to jail as a lesson not to commit a crime again.

Policemen and policewomen have the job of catching criminals so that they can be punished under the law.

See also *court of law, law, police,* and *prison.*

Crocodile

A crocodile is a large reptile with thick, tough skin. There are about 15 different kinds of crocodiles. They live in warm places all around the world. A crocodile likes to lie still in water. When a fish or animal swims by, the crocodile grabs it in its huge mouth. It drags its victim underwater to eat it. Crocodiles live near lakes and swamps and rivers. Only one kind, the saltwater crocodile, swims out into the ocean.

Crocodiles belong to an order of reptiles called Crocodilia. Alligators, caymans, and gavials are also members of this order.

See also *alligator*.

Crocodiles and other Crocodilia have the toughest skin of all animals.

Crocodiles have many teeth, but they can't chew. They swallow their food in large chunks.

Crusades

Many Crusaders fought in the name of religion. But other Crusaders wanted adventure or hoped to find great wealth.

The Crusades were Christian wars to free the Holy Land from Turkish rule.

The Holy Land of Palestine was sacred to Christians. Jesus had lived and died there. In the 11th century, the Muslim Turks conquered Palestine and other countries in the Middle East. In 1095, Pope Urban II asked Europe's religious leaders and nobles to drive the Turks from the Holy Land.

The Crusades lasted for nearly 200 years. The Crusaders captured Jerusalem on the First Crusade (1096–1099). But in the end the Crusades failed. By the close of the 13th century, the Turks had won back all of the land the Crusaders had captured.

The Crusades were wars for Christianity. Crusader knights wore crosses on their armor.

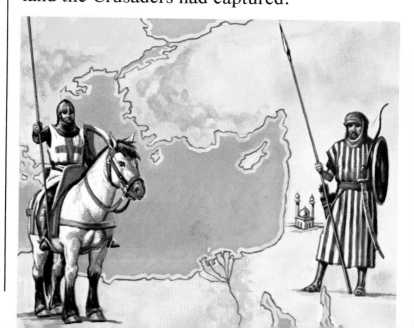

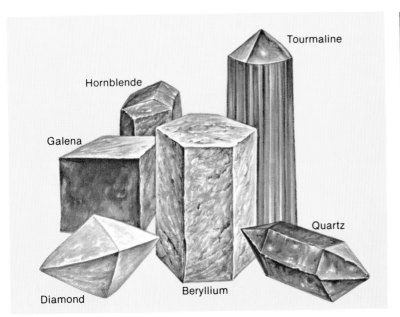

Tourmaline

Hornblende

Galena

Quartz

Diamond

Beryllium

Scientists know the exact shape of the crystals in different solids. This can help them identify an unknown substance.

Most solid materials like rocks and metals consist of crystals. Crystals are tiny solid bodies made up of atoms or molecules. Salt, sugar, ice, and diamonds are all made up of crystals. So are aspirin and wood. Many crystals are too small to see without a magnifying glass. But we can see some crystals, such as snowflakes.

Crystals can have many shapes. They may look like pyramids or boxes or cubes. Crystals of every shape always have flat sides. In some crystals the sides meet in right angles. In other crystals the sides meet in larger or smaller angles. Every crystal in a solid like a diamond has exactly the same shape as every other crystal in that solid. The diamond crystals fit together neatly to make a solid diamond.

Liquids and gases are not made of crystals. Their atoms and molecules are always moving around. In crystals, the atoms and molecules stay in one place.

See also *atoms and molecules*.

Curie, Marie and Pierre

Marie Curie is the only person ever to win a Nobel Prize for both chemistry and physics.

Marie (1867–1934) and Pierre (1859–1906) Curie were French scientists who discovered the element called radium. They also discovered that radium is radioactive. This means that it sends out rays. Other scientists have used radium to make many discoveries about the structure of the atom.

In 1903, the Curies, along with another French scientist, Henri Becquerel, received the Nobel Prize in physics for their work on radioactivity.

Marie Curie was born in Poland and came to Paris to study. She married Pierre in 1895. They worked together until Pierre died in 1906 when he was run over by a car. In 1911, Marie received a second Nobel Prize for her chemical studies of radium. She became director of the Pasteur Institute and also of the Curie Institute, founded to study the use of radium in the treatment of cancer.

See also *Nobel Prize* and *radiation*.

Cypress

Cypress trees are conifers. Like most conifers, they are evergreens and their leaves stay green all through the year. Cypress trees have flat leaves and grow seeds in small round cones.

Cypresses are found in North America, Central America, Asia, Europe, and Africa. There are about 20 different kinds or species. In America, the Monterey cypress is probably the most famous. It is found along the California coast and it can reach a height of 60 feet (18 m). The Monterey cypress has a flat top. Strong sea winds often bend its branches into strange shapes.

The bald cypress is really not a cypress. It belongs to a different family of trees. The bald cypress is found in wet places in the southeastern United States. Its roots are often covered with water. To get air, the roots sprout hollow tubes called "knees." These knees may rise 10 feet (3 m) above the surface of the water. Air passes down the tubes to the tree's roots.

See also *conifer* and *evergreens*.

Right: Wood from bald cypress trees does not rot in wet soil. It is used to make fence posts.

Left: The Monterey cypress is often planted as a lawn tree.

Dairy Products

Many kinds of cheese are aged before they are sold.

Dairy products are made from milk. Cows, sheep, and goats give milk. Their milk can be made into many products such as cheese, butter, yogurt, and ice cream. Milk that comes straight from a cow may have unhealthy germs in it. So it is pasteurized, or heated, to make it safe to drink. To get cream, milk is put into a machine that separates it into milk and cream.

Butter is made from cream. A machine called a churn shakes the cream until the fat in it becomes a solid. This solid is butter. It is washed and pounded until it becomes soft. Sometimes salt is added to it.

Cheese is made by adding a harmless germ to milk. The milk turns to curd. This curd is used to make cheeses. Yogurt is another dairy product made by adding bacteria or germs to milk. Ice cream is made from cream, milk, sugar, and flavorings.

Dairy products are healthy foods. Milk has almost everything in it that the body needs to grow.

A daisy is a flower that will grow almost anywhere. Daisies can be found in Europe, Asia, and the United States. Daisies are perennials. A perennial is a flower that grows year after year.

A daisy has a yellow or black "eye" at the center. Around the eye are white or yellow petals. Some daisies fold up or "close their eyes" at sunset. The name "daisy" comes from "day's eye," which refers to the sun.

The eye of a daisy is really made up of hundreds of tiny flowers called florets. These florets produce thousands of seeds. The seeds are spread by insects or the wind to start new daisy plants.

Daisies grow in warm places from late spring into early autumn.

The oxeye daisy has a yellow eye and white petals. The black-eyed susan has a black eye with yellow petals.

13

Dam

A dam is a barrier built on lakes, rivers, and streams. The dam holds back water or controls its flow. Beavers build dams using three trunks and branches. Today, engineers build dams using materials such as steel, concrete, stone, brick, or earth and rock.

Dams have been used by man to control water since the earliest civilizations. A dam may be built for a number of reasons. It may be built to make a lake or a reservoir. The reservoir stores drinking water for people and animals. It may be built to produce water power for making electricity. The force of the water is used to run machines called turbines that generate electricity. It may be built to provide water, or irrigation, for farming. Or it may be built to stop a body of water from flooding. Most large modern dams are built for several of these reasons.

See also *irrigation*.

America has many large dams, such as the Douglas Dam (above), which is part of the Tennessee Valley Authority.

Dance

Dance is the movement of the body in time to music or rhythms. In ancient times, people thought that when they danced they would please their gods. Then these gods would help them. For this reason, they had many special dances, such as hunting dances, war dances, and rain dances. People also danced to show that they were happy. They danced in groups at weddings and on holidays. This became known as folk dancing.

There are many different kinds of dance. Ballet dancing is very difficult. Social dancing is done for fun. The fox trot and the waltz are two kinds of social dance.

See also *ballet* and *modern dance*.

A ballet dancer has to learn special steps and movements.

Dancing makes people feel good.

Darwin, Charles

Many scientists and religious people did not agree with Charles Darwin when he published his theory of evolution.

Charles Darwin (1809–1882) was an English scientist who supplied proof for the theory of evolution. As a boy, Darwin was interested in nature and science. At college, he studied medicine but didn't like it. He took up religious studies instead. But he also studied botany, geology, and fossils.

In 1831, after his graduation from Cambridge, he went on a five-year scientific voyage around the world on the British naval ship H.M.S. *Beagle.* He collected fossils and studied the living animals he saw. This trip led Darwin to believe that all plants and animals had not been created at once. Instead, new species had evolved, or developed, and old ones had died out over a long period of time.

Darwin spent the next 20 years in England gathering more evidence to support evolution. In 1859, he published his famous book on evolution, *On the Origin of the Species.*

See also *evolution.*

Deafness

A person who is deaf is unable to hear sounds. People become deaf in two different ways. In one case, a person may be born deaf. In the other case, a person may be born with normal hearing and then become deaf, often from an illness or an accident.

People who are born deaf can learn how to talk. A person who has normal hearing learns to talk by copying what he or she hears other people say.

Deaf people learn to understand what people are saying by watching their actions and the movement of their lips. They can be taught to speak. But this is difficult. Schools for the deaf use special teachers and special equipment to teach their pupils.

Deaf people can also communicate without speaking. They can move their hands and bodies to make signs that stand for things or ideas. Or they can use finger spelling. Most deaf people use a combination of all of these methods to communicate.

In finger spelling, there is a finger sign for each letter of the alphabet.

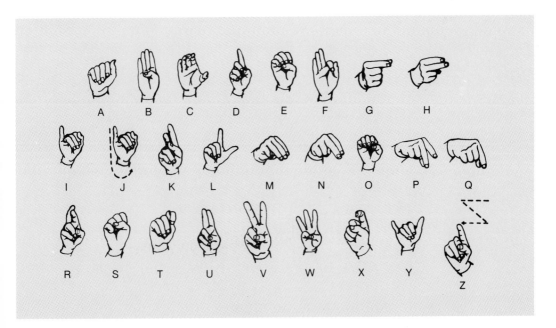

Death

Death is the end of life. All living things, plants, animals, and humans, live for a certain period of time, and then they die. A person dies when his or her heart and brain stop working.

Humans may die at any time from a disease or an accident. A very young person may die in this way. Most humans live until they reach a time of life called "old age." The signs of old age are gray hair, wrinkled skin, soft bones, and weak muscles. In old age, their bodies become weaker. Their weaker bodies also make it harder for them to get well again.

Most religions hold funeral services for the dead. Prayers are said for the person's soul. The person may be buried in a grave in the earth in a cemetery or in a vault. The grave is usually marked with a tombstone. Sometimes a dead person is cremated. The body is put in an oven, and the high temperature turns the body to ashes. The ashes are put in an urn for the person's relatives to keep.

See also *age*.

After death, people are buried in cemeteries. The gravestones shown here are hundreds of years old.

Deer

Deer are mammals related to cattle. They have feet with hoofs and most males grow antlers. There are more than 50 kinds of deer. The smallest is the South American pudu. It is only 12 inches (30 cm) tall. The largest is the moose. It can be seven feet (2.1 m) tall.

Male deer use their antlers to defend themselves against attack by other animals. Male deer also fight each other for a female. The male deer loses its antlers in autumn and grows new ones in the spring.

See also *antelope* and *moose*.

Like cattle, deer eat only plants and are ruminants. This means they chew their food several times before digesting it. Baby deer are called fawns.

Deer are very graceful. They can make high, twisting leaps in the air.

Depression

People without jobs sold apples on the street to make money during America's Great Depression.

A depression is a serious decline in the economy of a country. In a depression, many people are out of work. Many businesses close down. The economic activity of the country almost comes to a stop.

Economy is the word used to describe the total business activity in a country. This includes all of the businesses and all of the people who make things and provide services.

A depression develops over a period of time. It may begin when some companies close down because they are losing money. Their workers no longer have jobs and they have little or no money to buy things. Other companies may then close down because no one is buying what they sell. Over a period of time, many companies may close down and many workers may lose their jobs. There will then be a depression. In the 1930s, the United States had a serious depression called the Great Depression. It affected countries all over the world.

See also *economics*.

Desert

Land becomes a desert when there is not enough water for most plants to grow. Deserts are usually hot and dry. But some plants and animals can live in deserts. Cactuses and other hardy plants store the little water they get in their stems and leaves. Snakes and other reptiles also live in deserts. Even some people live in the desert. They move from place to place looking for food and water. They are called nomads.

There are also deserts in polar lands where it is very cold. The ground is frozen and there is very little water. Lichens, mosses, and other plants grow there only in the summer. Frozen deserts like this can be found in the northern parts of Asia and North America.

Death Valley is a famous desert in the United States. It is 282 feet (86 m) below sea level.

Sand dunes exist in many of the world's deserts.

Devil Ray

Devil rays often leap out of the water.

Devil rays are fish with large fins that look like wings. They are related to sharks. They can be 22 feet (6.7 m) across and weigh as much as 3,500 pounds (1,588 kg). They are also called manta rays.

When they swim, devil rays flap their fins up and down. The tail of a devil ray looks like a long, thin whip. Devil rays live in warm ocean water such as the Gulf Stream.

Devil rays usually swim near the surface of the sea. A devil ray may leap 15 feet (4.6 m) in the air. Then it may do a bellyflop back into the water. It lands with a loud slap that can be heard for miles.

Devil rays are gentle and do not attack swimmers. They have small, fairly flat teeth. They eat shellfish, small fish, and plankton, which consists of tiny plants and animals.

Devil rays do not lay eggs. They give birth to live babies, usually one at a time. A baby can weigh 30 pounds (14 kg).

See also *shark.*

Diamond

A diamond is a mineral. It is made up of the element called carbon. Diamond is the hardest known substance. Diamonds are very rare and valuable. They are used as gems in jewelry such as rings and necklaces. They are also used in industry to make drills and other grinding tools. Diamonds are only found in a rock called kimberlite. Rough diamonds are cut and polished to change them into bright white gems. Colored diamonds are not pure.

The weight of a diamond is given in carats. One carat equals about 1/142 ounce (200 mg).

See also *gems, jewelry,* and *mineral.*

Gem diamonds are cut to twinkle and sparkle with the colors of a rainbow.

The best diamonds have no flaws and no color. They are cut to reflect the most light.

Dickens, Charles

Charles Dickens (1812–1870) is one of the world's greatest writers. The stories and novels he wrote had exciting plots and many memorable characters. Among his most famous works are *Oliver Twist, A Tale of Two Cities,* and *A Christmas Carol.*

Dickens came from a poor family. At the age of 12 he had to go to work in a London factory. He later used his unhappy childhood experiences to create characters and scenes in many of his novels. *David Copperfield* is partly based on Dickens's life as a boy.

Dickens began writing at the age of 20 as a newspaper reporter. He also wrote humorous stories about the life in London for several magazines. These were included in his first book, *Sketches by Boz.* His second book, *Pickwick Papers,* was a great success and made him famous. He wrote other books and quickly became one of England's best-loved authors. He traveled around England and the United States reading his books to large audiences. Dickens's novels still seem real and true to life.

In the novel Oliver Twist, *Charles Dickens wrote about an orphan boy who had to beg for food and steal for a living.*

Digestive System

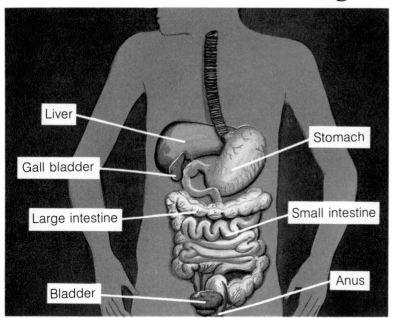

Liver

Stomach

Gall bladder

Large intestine

Small intestine

Bladder

Anus

The digestive system breaks down the food a person eats so that the body can use it. Digestion starts in the mouth. The teeth mash up the food. The juice in the mouth, called saliva, helps break it down. The food is then swallowed and goes to the stomach where it is churned and partly digested. Then the food goes into the small intestine. Here, juices from the pancreas and liver break down the food even more. These juices turn protein, fats, and carbohydrates into chemicals that the body's cells can absorb. Food that cannot be used passes out of the body.

The stomach is small when it is empty, but it can stretch to hold a lot of food.

Dinosaur

The front legs of the Gorgosaurus were useless. It walked and ran on its hind legs which were long and muscular.

Dinosaurs were reptiles that lived millions of years ago. Scientists have found dinosaur bones buried in the earth. They have discovered a great deal about dinosaurs by studying these bones.

The first large dinosaurs lived about 180 million years ago. The world was much warmer then and swamps covered much of the land. There were two groups of dinosaurs. One group ate plants, like Diplodocus. This dinosaur walked on all four legs and was about 90 feet (27 m) long. The other group ate meat, like Gorgosaurus. This dinosaur was about 30 feet (9.1 m) in length and stood on its hind legs. Gorgosaurus ate other dinosaurs.

Many plant-eating dinosaurs had armor to protect them from the meat-eating dinosaurs. One of these was Ankylosaurus. It was about 18 feet (5.5 m) long. Its back was covered with bony plates. These plates helped Ankylosaurus fool its enemies. When it sat down, it could be mistaken for a large rock.

Scientists don't know why all the dinosaurs died out. They do know that the earth became cooler and drier. This probably made it more difficult for dinosaurs to find food.

See also *Brachiosaurus, Brontosaurus, extinct animals, prehistoric reptile,* and *Tyrannosaurus.*

The Stegosaurus had raised plates on its back. These made it look bigger and fiercer to its enemies.

The Triceratops was a plant eater, but it looked very fierce.

Gorgosaurus was probably one of the last dinosaurs to die out about 75 million years ago.

Director

The director tells the actors and actresses how to play a scene.

Every movie and play has a director. The director is the person who controls how the film is made or how the play is presented.

The director guides the work of all the people who are part of the movie or the play. Among these people are the actors, the writers, the costumers, the makeup artists, and the stagehands. In the case of a movie, there will also be cameramen and film editors.

The director consults with all of these people and tells them his ideas about the play or movie. The director may ask the writer to make changes in the script. The director tells the actors and actresses how to play their parts. The director talks to the cameramen about how the movie will be photographed. In a movie, one part or scene may be filmed in different ways. The director and the film editor pick the scenes they like best. The director is concerned with how the play or film will look when it is seen by an audience.

See also *motion picture* and *play*.

Disasters can be caused by nature or by people.

A disaster is an event that usually happens unexpectedly and that causes great damage. A flood can send water across dry land. A plane crash or train wreck can kill many people. Storms, such as hurricanes and tornadoes, can carry away houses. A volcano that explodes can shower molten lava over the earth. Earthquakes can topple buildings.

After a disaster, governments and private organizations try to help people who have lost their homes or been injured. The Red Cross helps people all over the world. It takes care of those who are injured. It also provides food, clothes, and shelter for the homeless.

See also *flood, hurricane, Red Cross,* and *volcano.*

An earthquake can destroy houses and land and injure people.

Disease

Antibodies in the blood fight many diseases. Vaccination shots help the body to make antibodies.

A disease is a sickness. Pneumonia and influenza are two common diseases. A person who gets a disease will usually show signs, or symptoms, of it. A person with a cold will usually have a runny nose.

Some diseases are caused by germs or bacteria or viruses. These may be in food, water, or the air. And some diseases are caused by some part of the body, such as the heart, wearing out or breaking down.

People may be cured of a disease in various ways. The body makes antibodies that fight a disease. And a doctor may treat the disease with medicine such as an antibiotic.

See also *bacteria* and *vaccination*.

Diseases carried by germs are called infectious diseases. Germs are so small they can only be seen with a microscope.

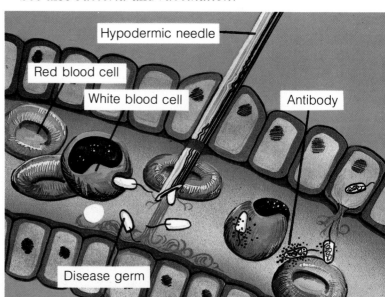

Hypodermic needle

Red blood cell

White blood cell

Antibody

Disease germ

Disney, Walt

Walt Disney (1901–1966) was the world's most popular and successful maker of cartoons. Among many other achievements, he made the first cartoon movie in color.

He started by making cartoon shorts starring Mickey Mouse and Donald Duck. He went on to make longer films such as *Snow White and the Seven Dwarfs, Fantasia, Pinocchio,* and *Bambi*. After World War II, animated movies or cartoons became expensive to produce. Disney then began to make films of true adventures, such as *The Living Desert*. He also created two famous amusement parks. He won a record 30 Academy Awards.

See also *animation*.

People come from all over to visit Disneyland in California and Disney World in Florida.

Mickey Mouse and Donald Duck are Walt Disney's two most famous cartoon characters.

Doctor

In an examination, doctors check a patient's reflexes by tapping the knees.

A doctor is someone who tries to make sick people healthy again. Doctors study for many years at medical schools. Some are trained to take care of sick people. Others are trained to do research on diseases and other problems.

A doctor examines a patient to find out why he or she feels sick. The doctor may make tests, such as a blood test, or take X rays.

There are many kinds of doctors. People who are sick or injured usually go to a general practitioner. This is a doctor who treats many kinds of illnesses. Pediatricians (pee-dee-ah-TRISH-unz) are experts at treating children. Surgeons perform operations.

See also *disease, medicine, surgery,* and *X ray.*

Doctors who are specialists treat a special part of the body, like the eyes, or a special disease, such as cancer.

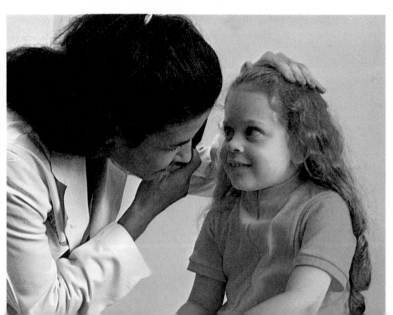

Dog

A dog is a four-legged, furry animal. Once all dogs lived in the wild as wolves do. About 10,000 years ago, dogs were domesticated, or tamed, by humans. Dogs were probably the first wild animals that became domesticated.

Dogs can hear and smell better than people. But a dog's vision is about the same as that of a human's.

There are more than 200 different breeds, or kinds, of dogs in the world today. Most are kept as pets. Some are small, like the chihuahua, which can weigh as little as 1½ pounds (68 grams). Others are very large, like the St. Bernard, which can weigh as much as 200 pounds (91 kg).

Several dogs received medals for carrying messages in wartime.

Dog owners should learn how to take good care of their pets to keep them healthy and happy.

Dolphin

One day people may learn to talk with dolphins.

Dolphins are mammals that live in the water. They are actually small whales, and they breathe air as whales and other mammals do. Dolphins live in all the oceans of the world and in Asian and South American rivers. Dolphins can grow to 14 feet (4.3 m) and weigh more than 500 pounds (227 kg). Dolphins can swim at a speed of close to 30 miles per hour (48 kph) and can leap high out of the water.

Dolphins are playful and intelligent animals. They communicate with each other by making various noises, such as barks, clicks, and whistles. Dolphins respond to people and sometimes let swimmers ride on their backs. Dolphins are often confused with porpoises, another kind of marine mammal. There are also dolphins that are fish. They are found in warm seas and are commonly called dorados.

Bottle-nosed dolphins like these are taught to perform tricks in aquariums.

Doodlebug

Doodlebugs are the young or larva of insects called lacewings. A doodlebug is a ferocious hunter. It has jaws that are like pliers.

To hunt ants and other insects, a doodlebug digs a hole in the sand. When an insect falls into the hole, the doodlebug grabs it in its jaws. Its jaws act like needles that inject the insect with a fluid. The fluid kills the insect. The doodlebug then sucks the insides from the insect's body.

When the doodlebug is ready to become an adult, it spins a cocoon over itself. It stays inside for a few weeks. When it comes out, it is an adult winged lacewing.

See also *insect* and *lacewing*.

The doodlebug's sharp jaws help it to catch and kill other insects.

Doodlebug is just one name for young lacewings. They are also called ant lions or aphid lions.

Dragon

In a famous legend, St. George kills a dragon and rescues a beautiful princess.

A dragon is an imaginary animal, not a real animal. No dragon ever lived. But there are many stories and legends about dragons. In these stories, dragons are large lizards with wings and the tail of a snake. Their heads look like the head of a crocodile. Their skin is scaly and their feet have lion's claws. They spit fire from their mouths.

In Western countries, dragons are thought of as monsters, which try to harm people. In China and other Asian countries, people believe that dragons are good and help mankind.

The Chinese celebrate their New Year by making paper dragons.

Dragonfly

Dragonflies are insects with long, thin bodies. They have large heads, huge eyes, and four lacy, transparent wings. There are nearly 3,000 kinds of dragonflies. They live near ponds, lakes, and swamps.

Dragonflies are fast fliers. Most of them fly at about 24 miles per hour (39 kph). Some can even fly as fast as 60 miles per hour (97 kph). Dragonflies can catch and eat mosquitoes, flies, and other insects while they are flying. Dragonflies have very good eyesight. Adult dragonflies have huge eyes. They can see something move when it is 50 feet (15 m) away.

Dragonflies lay eggs in water or on water plants. The young dragonflies that hatch from these eggs are called nymphs. Nymphs live underwater for one to five years. They eat insects and small fish. Then the nymphs climb out of the water. Their skins split open and the adult dragonfly comes out.

Some dragonflies lived 250 million years ago and had wings which measured over two feet (61 cm) from tip to tip. They were the largest insects that ever lived.

Dragonflies are useful because they eat pests such as mosquitoes and flies.

Drama

Drama consists of stories written for actors to perform on stage. The stories are called plays or dramas.

Drama probably began when early peoples acted out rituals to please their gods at harvest time and other special occasions. Drama is presented today to entertain, inform, and inspire audiences.

The first formal drama was presented in Greece in the 6th century B.C. Drama played an important role in Greek life. Greek dramatists like Euripides and Sophocles wrote plays of great emotional power. In the Middle Ages, most plays told biblical and other religious stories.

Dramas were first performed in theaters for paying audiences in England in the late 16th century. Shakespeare, the greatest dramatist of Western literature, acted with the company at the Globe theater in London and also wrote plays for it. Among the outstanding dramatists of more recent times are the Norwegian Henrik Ibsen and the Russian Anton Chekhov.

See also *actors; play; Shakespeare, William;* and *theater.*

Greek citizens watched dramas performed in amphitheaters like this one.

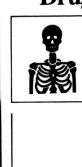

Drugs can be dangerous. Mr. Yuk is the new poison symbol which should warn children to stay away from them.

A drug is a chemical that affects the way the body works and is used to treat disease.

There are many different kinds of drugs and they affect the body in different ways. Some drugs, such as vitamins, may supply chemicals the body needs to work properly. Some drugs work on the entire body. Some drugs work on just one part of the body, such as the central nervous system, which is made up of the brain and the spinal column. Among the kinds of drugs that affect the central nervous system are tranquilizers, which relax a person, stimulants, which excite a person, and pain killers, which stop a person from feeling pain.

Some drugs do not work on the body itself. They fight germs that enter the body and cause diseases.

Drugs can be harmful if they are taken too often or in too large a dose. A person who takes a drug too often may become "addicted" to it. Then that person will feel sick unless he or she keeps on getting this drug.

See also *disease; medicine; Salk, Jonas; vaccination;* and *vitamin.*

Drum

The drum is very important in African and Latin American music.

A drum is a kind of musical instrument called a percussion instrument. Some other percussion instruments are pianos, cymbals, bells, and tambourines.

A drum is made of a membrane, or skin, stretched tightly over a frame, which is usually round. It is played by beating the membrane with sticks, called drumsticks, or fingers, or other objects.

The kettledrum is the most important drum in an orchestra. Some other drums in orchestras and bands are the snare drum, the bass drum, and the tenor drum.

Percussion instruments can be as small as a bell or as large as a bass drum.

Duck

Ducks are birds that can swim. They are related to geese and swans. They have large bodies, short legs, webbed feet, and flat bills. Ducks are found all over the world except in the Antarctic.

There are many different kinds of ducks. The largest kinds grow to a length of 30 inches (76 cm) and can weigh 16 pounds (7.3 kg). Ducks have feathers that are made waterproof by oil. This oil comes from a gland in their tail.

Ducks are strong fliers. Some can fly as fast as 70 miles per hour (113 km). They migrate over long distances when the weather gets cold. Most ducks are wild. But tame ducks are raised for their meat and eggs.

Male ducks usually have brighter-colored feathers than females.

Mallard ducks protect their young until they are old enough to care for themselves.

Eagle

Eagles may return to the same nest every year. They add more sticks to make them bigger.

Eagles are large birds with powerful wings and very good eyesight. An eagle can see a small animal from high in the sky. The eagle swoops down quickly. It grabs the animal with its sharp claws and kills it with its hooked beak. Eagles hunt birds, fish, snakes, lizards, and small mammals.

Eagles build large nests made of twigs and sticks on high rocks and cliffs, and in tall trees. The largest bird's nest known was built by bald eagles. This nest was 9.5 feet (2.9 m) wide and 20 feet (6.1 m) deep. The bald eagle is the national emblem of the United States. There are about 55 different kinds of eagles and they are found in most regions of the world.

Baby eagles have large eyes and fluffy feathers.

Ears and Eyes

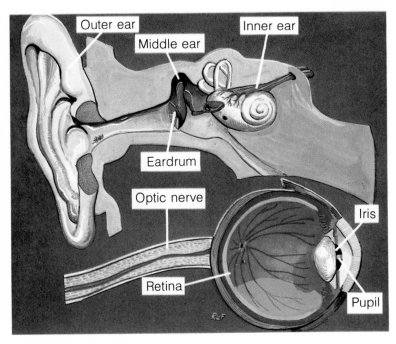

Outer ear
Middle ear
Inner ear
Eardrum
Optic nerve
Iris
Retina
Pupil

This diagram shows the important parts of the ear and the eye.

The ears and eyes are the organs of the body that make it possible to hear and see.

Sound is caused by vibrations that travel in waves. From the outer ear, these waves move down a channel to the eardrum. The waves make the eardrum vibrate, and it passes the vibrations on to three small bones in the middle ear. The bones vibrate to pass the sound on to the inner ear. Liquid in the inner ear picks up the vibrations. Cells in the inner ear sense the vibrations and send nerve impulses to the brain. The brain turns the impulses into the sounds a person hears.

Light enters the eye through the pupil. This is the dark circle in the center of the iris, the colored part of the eye. Behind the iris is a lens. The lens focuses the light on the retina at the back of the eye. Nerve cells in the retina send signals to the brain through the optic nerve. The brain organizes the signals so that a person sees.

Earth

This is how the earth looks from space. One astronaut described it as "a big blue marble."

The earth is the fifth largest of the nine planets in the solar system and the one on which human beings live. The earth is an almost sphere-shaped ball about 7,920 miles (12,743 km) in diameter. About 29 percent of the earth's total area of 197 million square miles (510 million sq km) is land. The rest of the earth's area is covered with oceans and seas.

The earth's interior consists of three major layers. The inner layer is the core. It is about 4,300 miles (6,919 km) in diameter, and it is believed to consist mainly of nickel and iron. They are at such high temperatures that they are liquid, though scientists believe that at the center of the core there is a ball of solid iron. Wrapped around the core is a mantle of solid rock that is about 1,800 miles (2,896 km) thick. Above this is the earth's crust, also made of solid rock. It is about 20 miles (32 km) thick under the continents and about three miles (4.8 km) thick under the oceans.

See also *geology*.

Earthquake

An earthquake is a movement of the ground caused by the movement of rock inside the earth. An earthquake can be 10,000 times as powerful as an atomic bomb. The force of a strong earthquake can make the ground move and shake and even split it open. Buildings may fall down. People may be hurt or killed. Often, an earthquake breaks electric and gas lines. This may start fires. Fires often are the greatest danger in an earthquake.

In 1906, a large earthquake struck San Francisco and most of the city was destroyed. In 1976, an earthquake in China killed more than 240,000 people.

Scientists can measure how strong earthquakes are with an instrument called a seismograph. Some earthquakes take place just beneath the surface of the earth. Others take place 450 miles (724 km) down. There may be as many as one million earthquakes each year but only a very few cause great damage.

An earthquake can split the earth open and cause buildings to fall.

Earwig

FAMILY COUNSELOR

Earwigs live together in friendly family groups.

Earwigs are insects with long pincers at the back end of their bodies. They use these pincers to protect themselves from enemies. Earwigs have front and rear wings. The rear wings fold under the front ones. It is difficult for an earwig to fold up its wings in this way. Probably for this reason, earwigs do not fly very often.

There are about 1,000 kinds of earwigs. They live under bark, stones, logs, and trash. Some live among flower petals.

Earwigs stay hidden during the day and come out to look for food at night. Earwigs eat plants, flies, caterpillars, and other insects.

Most insects leave their eggs alone after laying them. But the female earwig puts her eggs in a hole and guards them. She licks the eggs to keep them warm, wet, and clean.

People used to believe that earwigs would crawl into ears. This is not true.

Easter is an important holiday of the Christian religion. Jesus was crucified and died on the cross on Good Friday. He was placed in a tomb and Christians believe that he then rose from this tomb on Easter Sunday. In the Christian religion, this is known as the Resurrection.

The date of Easter changes each year. It comes on a Sunday after March 21 and before April 26. There are about six weeks of Lent that come before Easter. Lent is a time of fasting and prayer.

Many people celebrate Easter as the beginning of spring.

See also *Christianity* and *Jesus Christ*.

People decorate eggs to show their joy in Easter and the coming of spring.

For the Easter parade, people dress up in their best clothes.

Eastern Culture

Acrobats dressed in traditional Chinese costumes play roles in Chinese operas.

Peoples in Eastern lands, such as India, China, and Japan, have their own special cultures. Their art, music, drama, literature, and architecture are often quite different from those of the West. And they are often different from each other. The music of India and China does not sound like Western music, which normally has an eight-note scale. Chinese music uses a five-note scale, and Indian melodies are based on irregular patterns of notes called ragas.

See also *Asia, China, India,* and *Japan.*

Indian musicians use Indian instruments to play Indian music.

Eastern Europe

Eastern Europe includes the countries of East Germany, Poland, Hungary, Rumania, Bulgaria, Czechoslovakia, Yugoslavia, and Albania. All of these countries came under the strong influence of the Soviet Union after World War II. All now have communist governments and all except Albania and Yugoslavia are part of the Soviet bloc.

About 140 million people live in Eastern Europe. Most of them belong to the Roman Catholic Church. The Soviet Union has tried to discourage religious worship, but the church is still a powerful force. Agriculture is the major economic activity. Among the crops grown are rye, potatoes, wheat, corn, tobacco, and rice. The Eastern European countries have tried to industrialize their economies and they produce a variety of manufactured goods.

See also *Europe* and the *Soviet Union*.

Warsaw, shown here, is the capital of Poland and one of the largest cities in Eastern Europe. The largest city is Budapest, the capital of Hungary.

Eclipse

During a total eclipse of the sun, the sky darkens. It can last from just a few seconds to 7½ minutes.

In an eclipse a heavenly body becomes dark temporarily. In an eclipse of the sun, the moon comes between the earth and sun. The moon blocks out light from the sun. This is called a solar eclipse. When the eclipse is total, only a brilliant ring of light can be seen around the sun.

The other eclipse is an eclipse of the moon, called a lunar eclipse. It takes place when the earth comes between the sun and moon. The earth's shadow cuts off light from the sun and the moon appears dark. A lunar eclipse can last up to one hour and 50 minutes.

It is very dangerous to look right at an eclipse of the sun. The sun's rays can hurt the eyes.

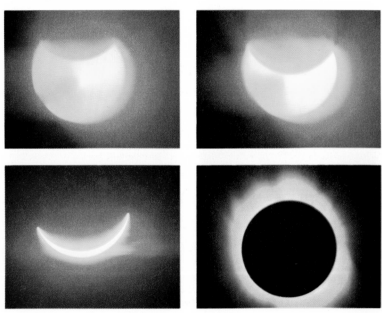

Ecology (e-COL-ogy) is the study of how living things are related to each other and to their environment, the place where they live. Ecology is also concerned with what man does to the environment, such as polluting the air or water. Scientists who study these matters are called ecologists.

Ecology comes from two Greek words meaning "study of the home, or surroundings." Their environment provides living things with what they need to live and grow. This includes food and energy, water, and living space. Living things, in turn, become a part of their environment. Plants supply food for certain animals. These animals are eaten by other animals in a food chain. Dead plants and animals decay and return nourishment to the soil. This helps new plants to grow. In this way, living and nonliving things in an environment interact to create a complex web of life.

See also *conservation, food chain,* and *pollution.*

Wasps interact with their environment by pollinating flowers, which helps new plants to grow. Some wasps also help plants to survive by eating insects that attack these plants.

Economics

Economics is the science that deals with the manufacture, distribution, and use of goods and services. Scientists who study these activities are called economists.

The economic system of a country is called its economy. Some countries have a capitalist economy and others have a communist economy. A capitalist economy can be thought of as a giant marketplace in which millions of people make, sell, and buy things. Economists want to know the answers to questions such as: how many people are working; what kind of jobs they have; how much money they make; and how much they produce. The economies of modern countries are very complicated. Millions of people do work that is part of the total economic activity of the country. Economists use computers to keep track of all this economic activity.

Economics has become an important modern science. If the economy is not working well and many people are out of work, the economist is asked to find out what the problem is and how to solve it.

See also *depression, Industrial Revolution,* and *money.*

In a modern economy, goods are produced in great quantities in factories and sold all over the country in stores like this supermarket.

Edison, Thomas

Edison held more than 1,000 United States patents for his inventions.

Thomas Alva Edison (1847–1931) was one of the greatest inventors who ever lived.

As a boy, Edison displayed great curiosity. He did not like school and was educated at home by his mother. He went to work when he was 12 and soon began to dream of being an inventor. He got his first patent in 1868. He opened a laboratory in Menlo Park, New Jersey where he was able to develop and test his new ideas. Perhaps Edison's greatest inventions were the phonograph, the perfection of the electric light bulb, and the motion picture camera. All of these led to the founding of huge industries.

Edison perfected the light bulb and also a system to use electric lighting in homes and offices.

Education

Students often come back to visit their teachers.

Education is the process by which people learn. Formal education usually takes place in schools. But people are also educated informally. People learn things outside of school, from their parents, friends, TV, and the world around them.

Formal education in school begins with reading and writing. It would be difficult for a person to learn other subjects, such as mathematics, history, or art, without knowing how to read and write. The goal of education is to teach a person how to think and reason and solve problems. In this way, a person learns to use knowledge in solving the problems of life.

See also *school*.

Formal education begins when a student learns how to read and write.

Little fish called wrasses clean moray eels of pests.

Eels are fish that look like snakes. They usually have one long fin that runs from their head to their tail. Eels can be found in both fresh and salt water. Saltwater eels eat fish, crabs, and other sea animals. Freshwater eels eat fish, insects, and frogs.

Saltwater eels live all of their lives in the sea. European and American freshwater eels migrate to the sea to lay their eggs. They travel thousands of miles, and always go to the same place, the Sargasso Sea in the Atlantic Ocean. The female lays about 20 million eggs. The male fertilizes them. Then both parents die. The young eels that hatch travel to the same rivers and ponds in Europe and America where their parents lived.

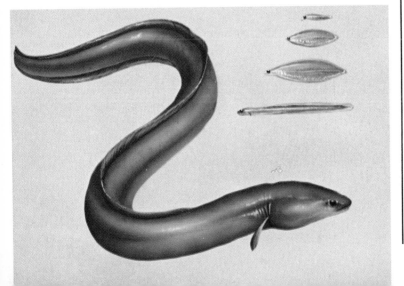

It takes European freshwater eels three years to return to their home waters from the Sargasso Sea. American freshwater eels make this trip in about one year.

55

Egg

People eat eggs that are laid by hens and other animals, such as ducks.

An egg is a special cell that is formed in the body of a female animal. Young animals develop from the eggs. Most fish, birds, snakes, insects, and alligators hatch from eggs. Many fish and amphibians lay their tiny eggs in jellylike masses in water.

Most of the egg is food for the developing animal that grows inside the egg. The developing animal is called an embryo (EM-bree-oh). The egg is protected by a tough outer coating. Sometimes this coating is a hard shell.

In mammals, babies grow from eggs which remain inside the mothers' bodies.

Eggs are decorated at Easter time. In some parts of the world, they are given as presents.

Egrets and Herons

Egrets and herons are birds with long legs and long bills that live near the shallow waters of rivers, marshes, lakes, and seas. There are about 60 kinds of herons. Egrets are one kind.

Egrets and herons are found on all the continents of the world except Antarctica. Most egrets and herons feed on fish, insects, and other small animals that live in or near the water. Most egrets and herons have long, curving necks. When they fly, they retract their necks into an S shape and hold their legs straight out behind them. Egrets are usually white in color, but sometimes the white has flashes of darker-colored feathers. Herons also may be white, but most are either blue, gray, or brown, or a combination of these colors.

Some egrets sit on the backs of cattle and other grazing animals. They eat the insects that come close to these animals.

Herons and egrets were once hunted for their decorative feathers, which grow during the mating season. They are now protected by law in many countries.

57

Egypt, Ancient

The tombs of Egyptian kings, such as King Tutankhamen, contained furniture, statues, and other items of value intended for use after death.

Ancient Egypt became a united country about 3100 B.C. It was a powerful kingdom for the next 2,000 years, until about 1000 B.C. Its civilization was an advanced one. Egyptians invented one of the first calendars. They also used one of the first written alphabets. This was a form of picture-writing called hieroglyphics. The ancient Egyptians also made one of the earliest forms of paper, called papyrus. The kings of Egypt, called pharaohs, built great tombs for themselves. The most famous of these were the pyramids. The Egyptians believed in a life after death, and pharaohs filled their tombs with objects.

See also *ancient civilizations* and *pyramid*.

The Great Sphinx at Giza has the body of a lion and the head of King Khafre. It was carved about 2600 B.C. His pyramid is behind it.

Albert Einstein (INE-stine) (1879–1955) was one of the greatest scientists who ever lived. He was born of Jewish parents in Germany. As a boy, he didn't like school. But he studied math and science at home. He went to college in Zurich, Switzerland, and studied physics. In 1905, he published a new theory on the nature of the universe, the special theory of relativity. It explains how matter, energy, and time are related. This theory of relativity made Einstein world famous and in 1921 he received the Nobel Prize in physics.

Einstein became an American citizen and taught and studied at the Institute for Advanced Study in Princeton, New Jersey.

As a boy Einstein was a poor student and did not like going to school.

Electric Eel

Electric eels "talk" to each other with electric waves.

Electric eels are fish, but they do not belong to the eel family. Their long bodies are mostly tail. This makes them look like eels. Electric eels average between three and seven feet (0.9–2.1 m) in length. They live in freshwater rivers in South America.

Electric eels can produce more than 500 volts of electricity. This is enough to light a neon bulb. They make electricity using certain muscles in their body. With this electricity they shock fish and frogs and then eat them. They also use electricity to find their way in dark water. If the electrical waves they send out hit an object, the eel knows it and swims around the object.

Electric eels look for mates by sending out electrical signals.

Electricity is a form of energy. Electricity occurs throughout nature. Lightning is a discharge of electrical energy. Animals produce electrical impulses in their bodies which carry signals to their brains and other organs. And atoms are held together in molecules by electrical energy.

Humans use electrical energy for many purposes. Electricity runs the motors in most factories. It also makes possible electric lighting, electric appliances, and inventions like the telephone.

Electricity can be produced by machines called generators. The current that is produced flows through wires that are good conductors of electricity. Electric current is basically made up of a flow of electrons. Metals that are good conductors allow these electrons to flow easily. Other metals resist the flow of electrons and become hot and glow. Metals with high resistance are used in electric light bulbs and appliances such as the toaster.

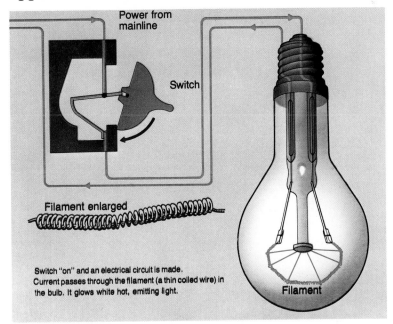

Power from mainline

Switch

Filament enlarged

Switch "on" and an electrical circuit is made.
Current passes through the filament (a thin coiled wire) in
the bulb. It glows white hot, emitting light.

Filament

The thin wire in a bulb glows and creates light because it resists the flow of electric current passing through it.

Electronic Music

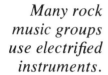

Many rock music groups use electrified instruments.

Electronic music is composed and played on special electronic machines called synthesizers. These machines can make almost any sound. They can sound like musical instruments, or they can make very different sounds. Basically, these machines operate like computers.

Only one person is needed to operate an electronic music machine. This person sits in a special recording studio and uses the machine to create electronic music. The music is recorded on tape. When the tape is played back, it can be played faster or slower or even backward. And sounds from nature or nonmusical sounds can be added to the tape.

A composer of electronic music can sit at a keyboard and press buttons to make sounds electronically.

Electronics

Electronics is the science that deals with the movement of electrons. Electrons are particles in atoms. Their movement produces an electric current. Scientists are able to regulate and control the flow of electrons by using devices such as the electron tube and the transistor. The science of electronics has made possible many inventions that are highly important in modern life, including TV, computers, and many scientific and industrial instruments.

See also *computer, electricity, radio, telephone,* and *television.*

Modern electronic devices like these can be made smaller by using tiny transistors instead of electron tubes.

The picture tube in a TV set controls the flow of electrons to create a picture. When the flow is interfered with in some way, the picture becomes unclear.

Element

Every element is given an atomic number according to the number of protons each of its atoms has in its nucleus. For example, the atomic number of copper is 29. Every atom of copper taken from this copper mine has 29 protons in its nucleus.

Elements are the basic chemical substances from which everything in the universe is made. An element cannot be broken down into a simpler substance by ordinary chemical means. Compounds which contain more than one element can be broken down into the separate elements from which they are made. There are 106 known elements.

Some elements are solids, such as iron. Others are gases, such as helium. And others are liquids at room temperature, such as mercury.

Every element is made up of its own kind of atom. Atoms are particles too small to be seen even with a microscope. Atoms are made up of even smaller particles. The three most important of these are the proton, the neutron, and the electron. Each atom has a center or nucleus where the protons and neutrons are held together. The rest of the atom is made up of electrons. Electrons have a negative charge and protons have a positive charge.

Elephant

Elephants are the largest mammals that live on land. There are two kinds of elephant. One lives in Africa. The other lives in India and other parts of Asia. The African bush elephant is the largest of these. Large bush males are about 11.5 feet (3.5 m) high at the shoulder and weigh about 6 tons (5.4 mt).

Indian and African elephants do not look alike. One noticeable difference is that African elephants have larger ears. All elephants have trunks and all males have ivory tusks.

Elephants are very strong and intelligent. They were probably tamed about 3500 B.C. They have been used to perform work and for riding. They have very good memories and seldom forget a command or a trick once they have learned it.

At birth a young elephant weighs about 200 pounds (91 kg).

African elephants (left) and Indian elephants both eat plants, fruit, and nuts, and they usually travel in herds of 25 to 30 animals.

65

Elizabeth I

Elizabeth encouraged voyages of exploration and colonization. During her reign, Sir Francis Drake made a three-year voyage around the world.

Elizabeth I (1533–1603) was one of England's most outstanding rulers. Under her rule, England became a leading power.

Elizabeth was the daughter of Henry VIII and Anne Boleyn. She was well educated and intelligent. She became queen in 1558 and reigned until her death in 1603. Her major goal was to promote the unity of her country. She did much to lessen the violent conflict between Protestants and Catholics that began when Henry VIII broke with the Roman Catholic Church and made the English Anglican Church independent of Rome. She encouraged trade and industry that brought prosperity to the country. And she guided England through its long war against Spain, in which England established its naval superiority by defeating the Spanish Armada in 1588. She was also a patron of the arts, and during her years on the throne, English writers, such as William Shakespeare, produced great literature.

The elm is a tall tree that is often planted as a shade tree. The American elm or white elm is the most common kind in America. It grows to be about 80 to 120 feet (24–37 m) tall. It is usually found in eastern America. Other kinds of elms grow in England, Scotland, Siberia, and China. The wood of elm tree is hard and does not split easily. It is used to build ships and to make furniture and barrels.

Many elm trees have been killed by Dutch elm disease. This disease is carried by bark beetles. In 50 years, it has killed about 10 million elm trees in the United States.

Homeowners like elm trees because their delicate leaves make raking easier.

The bark beetle eats the bark at the base of elm twigs and thus spreads the fungus which causes Dutch elm disease.

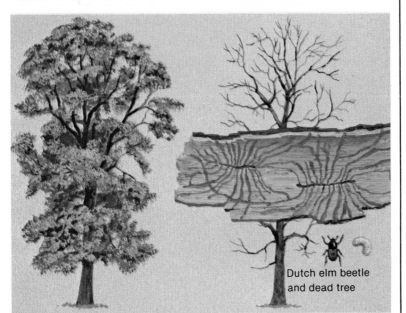

Dutch elm beetle and dead tree

Energy

Energy is the ability to do work. Electricity, heat, and fuels such as oil are all sources of energy. The work that scientists refer to when they speak of energy is physical work, not the mental effort of solving a problem. Scientists define work as the amount of energy necessary to move something a certain distance. Lifting a weight a foot above the ground requires a certain amount of work. Lifting the same weight twice as high requires twice as much work.

Scientists describe energy as kinetic energy and potential energy. Kinetic energy is energy produced by motion. For example, if a weight is dropped on a post to drive it into the ground, the moving weight as it falls has kinetic energy. Before the weight is dropped and while it is still at rest, it has potential energy. Potential energy refers to work that can be done in the future, for example, by the weight when it is dropped.

See also *chemistry, electricity, fuel,* and *heat.*

Engine

A steam engine provides the power that turns the paddlewheel on a paddle-wheel boat.

An engine is a machine that uses energy to perform work. The energy may come from the wind, or from water, or from heat. Heat engines are the most common kind of engine. They get their energy by burning a fuel, such as wood, coal, oil, or gas.

Engines did not come into widespread use until James Watt perfected the steam engine. The steam engine could perform enormous amounts of work mechanically.

See also *steam engine* and *Industrial Revolution*.

The human body is a kind of engine. It uses the energy it gets from food to do its work.

Engineering

Civil engineers work from detailed plans in building such projects as dams.

Engineering is the work of inventing, designing, and building the machines and structures that make up our modern civilization. There are many different kinds of engineers. For example, civil engineers are mainly concerned with building such things as roads, dams, buildings, and bridges. Among the other important kinds of engineers are mechanical, chemical, electrical, industrial, metallurgical, and agricultural engineers.

See also *bridge, construction, dam,* and *tunnel.*

In building a tunnel, engineers may plan the construction so that digging starts at each end and meets in the middle.

Entertainment

Entertainment is any performance or spectacle that amuses or interests an audience. Entertainment relaxes people and takes them away from their everyday life. It may make them laugh, cry, or fill them with amazement. Entertainment can take many different forms. Films, TV, stage plays and musicals, and sporting events are all entertainment. So are concerts, operas, and dance performances.

Entertainment today is a very big business. Radio, television, sports, and the theater are leading entertainment industries.

See also *motion picture, music, opera, play, radio,* and *television.*

Listening to the radio can make a person forget everyday problems.

Opera is a colorful and exciting form of entertainment.

Erosion

Erosion is the wearing away of the earth's rocks and its dirt or topsoil. Wind and water are the two main forces that cause erosion. Wind blows away loose dirt and sand. Water runs down hills and carries soil into rivers and streams. Ocean waves wear down rocks on the coast and carry pebbles and soil from beaches out into the sea. Rivers erode the rock along their banks. Glaciers cut into the soil and rock of a landscape. They also push up rocks and carry them along as they move.

Most erosion takes place very slowly. Waves may take hundreds of years to wear down a rock. But people often speed up erosion. They cut down trees that hold the soil together and they plow up grass or let animals eat too much of it.

Farmers are learning how to stop erosion. They plant trees to break the wind. They plow in curves instead of in straight lines.

See also *conservation*.

Sculptured rock formations, like these in Utah, are the result of erosion.

Eskimos wear heavy jackets or parkas to keep them warm in the Arctic cold.

Eskimos or Inuits are people who live in Alaska, Canada, Greenland, and Siberia. Eskimos are a separate race. They are most like the Mongols of eastern Asia. Eskimos have lived in the extreme cold of the far north for hundreds of years and many still follow ancient customs.

Eskimos find food by hunting and fishing. They eat fish, birds, seals, caribou, musk oxen, polar bears, whales, and walruses. They make their clothes out of caribou skin because it is warm and lightweight. They travel by dog sled or by boats made of animal skins. These boats are called kayaks and umiaks.

In recent years, some Eskimos have given up their old way of life. These Eskimos no longer live in sod houses made of earth and logs or in snowhouses in the winter and in tents in the summer. They live in modern homes and they send their children to school. They travel by snowmobile instead of dog sled, and they hunt with rifles instead of harpoons.

See also *Arctic*.

Europe

ICELAND

NORWAY

FINLAND

SWEDEN

SOVIET UNION

NORTH SEA

DENMARK

BALTIC SEA

IRELAND

GREAT BRITAIN

EAST GERMANY

POLAND

① WEST GERMANY

②

ATLANTIC OCEAN

③

FRANCE

CZECHOSLOVAKIA

④

AUSTRIA

HUNGARY

⑤

RUMANIA

⑥

⑦

YUGOSLAVIA

⑧ ITALY

BULGARIA

PORTUGAL

SPAIN

ALBANIA

GREECE

MEDITERRANEAN SEA

⑨

① NETHERLANDS

② BELGIUM

③ LUXEMBOURG

④ LIECHTENSTEIN

⑤ SWITZERLAND

⑥ ANDORRA

⑦ SAN MARINO

⑧ MONACO

⑨ MALTA

Europe is one of the seven continents. It has 34 countries with a total population of around 690 million people. One of these countries, the Soviet Union, is the largest in the world. But only about one-half of the Soviet Union is included in Europe. The other half is in Asia.

The Arctic Ocean lies to the north of the European continent and the Mediterranean Sea to the south. Europe's western coastline is on the Atlantic Ocean. Its eastern boundary is the Ural Mountains in the Soviet Union.

The people of Europe speak about 30 different languages, such as French, German, Italian, Spanish, and Russian. Most Europeans are Christians.

Modern industries and factories began in Europe in the 18th century. European countries sold their products all over the world. This brought great wealth to many European countries.

Europe is the birthplace of Western civilization. Many priceless treasures are in museums, such as the Louvre in Paris, France, and the Prado in Madrid, Spain. Europe also has masterpieces of architecture, such as the ancient Greek and Roman temples and the cathedrals or churches of the Middle Ages. Many of the world's greatest artists have been European, including Michelangelo, Rembrandt, Cézanne, and Picasso. Europe has also produced great writers like Shakespeare, Dickens, Dostoevski, and Balzac.

Great portions of Europe were destroyed during World War I (1914–1918) and World War II (1939–1945). But its cities and factories were rebuilt. Today, it remains a great center of industry and civilization.

See also *Eastern Europe, France, Germany, Great Britain, Ireland, Italy, Scandinavia,* and *Spain.*

The gondolas of Venice are just one way Europeans travel. The countries of Europe are linked to one another by modern transportation, including airlines, railroads, and highways.

Evergreens

Many houses are made from evergreen wood.

Evergreens are plants that keep their leaves all year long. Some evergreens, like holly and mountain laurel, have thick, wide leaves. They are called broad-leaved evergreens. Other evergreens like spruce, pine, and fir have needlelike leaves. They are called narrow-leaved evergreens. In the summer an evergreen can have old leaves and fresh new leaves on the same twig. Many kinds of evergreens have cones that contain seeds. Many birds and animals like to eat these seeds.

Evergreen trees are widely planted. They are attractive because they stay green all year. Evergreen wood is used for many things, such as building houses and other structures.

Narrow-leaved evergreens like these are often used for Christmas trees.

Evolution

Evolution is the theory that humans, animals, and plants have developed, or evolved, from earlier and more primitive forms of life. Charles Darwin, an English scientist, first offered evidence for the theory of evolution.

Evolution explains how life developed on earth. At first, there was no life at all. Then tiny plants appeared in the sea. Tiny sea animals followed. Fishes then evolved from the simpler sea animals. Some animals started to breathe air and crawled onto land. They became the first amphibians. Reptiles like lizards evolved from amphibians. Later, some reptiles evolved into birds and mammals. Scientists believe that apelike mammals are the evolutionary relatives of humans.

These changes took place over millions of years. Animals and plants changed, or adapted, to new ways of life in order to survive. Some plants and animals could not adapt and died off.

The horse evolved to its present form over a period of 60 million years.

EVOLUTION OF THE HORSE

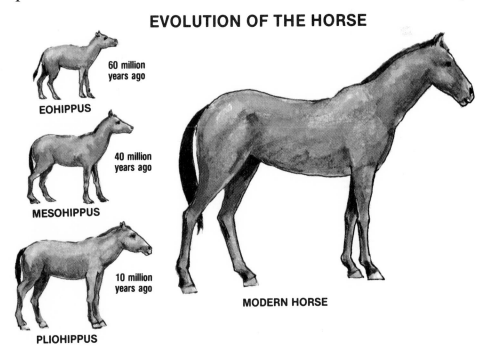

60 million years ago

EOHIPPUS

40 million years ago

MESOHIPPUS

10 million years ago

PLIOHIPPUS

MODERN HORSE

Exploration

The Phoenicians became a great sea power beginning about 1200 B.C. and traveled across the Mediterranean to Spain, Sicily, and North Africa.

Exploration is the act of traveling to an unfamiliar place and discovering what it is like. Curiosity, a desire for adventure, and economic gain are the major reasons why man has ventured from familiar to unknown lands.

The first explorers whose travels are recorded were the Egyptians, Phoenicians, Carthaginians, and Greeks. They explored the area of the Mediterranean Sea, which was their home. They also traveled east into Asia, south down the coast of Africa to Cape Verde, and west into the Atlantic Ocean. Alexander the Great reached Afghanistan and northern India. The Romans traveled to Britain and Germany and established land and sea routes to China in the 1st century A.D. In the 9th and 10th centuries, the Vikings colonized Iceland and Greenland and then reached the coast of Newfoundland in North America. The Crusades in the Middle East made many Europeans look to Asia as a source of wealth. Marco Polo, a Venetian, traveled to China in

Columbus set sail from Spain to discover a new sea route to Asia. Instead, he opened up America to European exploration.

the 13th century.

Still, at the beginning of the 15th century, most of the world was unknown to Europeans. Most only knew the parts of Asia and Africa that bordered on the Mediterranean Sea. The Americas, the Pacific, most of Africa, and the Arctic and Antarctic regions were uncharted. About 1400, an era of exploration began that led to the exploration of all these unknown regions.

See also *Alexander the Great; explorer; Polo, Marco; Roman empire;* and *Vikings.*

The Vikings braved the dangers of the north Atlantic and made many voyages to North America.

Explorer

A great age of exploration by Europeans began about 1400. The sea explorers of this time had the advantage of better ships and better navigation devices than the sailors before them. The tiny country of Portugal supplied more than its share of great explorers. Others came from Italy, France, Spain, and England.

Vasco da Gama, a Portuguese, made the first sea voyage around Africa in 1497. Da Gama sailed around the Cape of Good Hope at Africa's tip and continued on into the Indian Ocean. He arrived at the trading center of Calicut in India in May 1498. Da Gama's voyage finally gave Europe the sea passage to the east that it had long wanted. Five years before, Christopher Columbus had sailed west to find that passage and discovered the New World instead. After Columbus, other men explored the New World. One of these was an Italian, Amerigo Vespucci, who probably explored the northern and eastern coasts of South America in 1499. America is named after

Routes of some of the leading explorers are shown on this map.

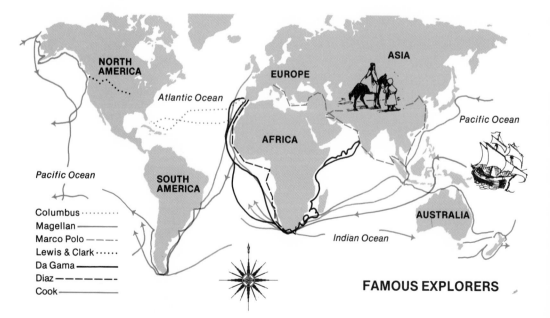

NORTH AMERICA

ASIA

EUROPE

Atlantic Ocean

Pacific Ocean

AFRICA

Pacific Ocean

SOUTH AMERICA

Columbus ··········
Magellan ————
Marco Polo — — — -
Lewis & Clark ······
Da Gama ————
Diaz — — — — —
Cook ————

AUSTRALIA

Indian Ocean

FAMOUS EXPLORERS

him. The first voyage around the world was led by Ferdinand Magellan, a Portuguese sailor whose ships flew the Spanish flag.

The Pacific Ocean was explored during the 16th, 17th, and 18th centuries. In the 17th century, the Spanish, Dutch, and English made voyages to the Pacific. It was Captain James Cook, an Englishman, who largely filled in the map of that ocean. Cook made three voyages between 1768 and 1778. He was killed in the Hawaiian Islands, which he discovered. He also visited Tahiti and Australia.

In the mid-19th century, Africa was still known as the "Dark Continent." The coasts were known to Europeans, but the center of Africa remained unexplored until a Scottish medical missionary, David Livingstone, explored it. Livingstone wrote about Africa and other explorers followed him.

Explorers did not reach the North and South poles until the 20th century. In 1909, an American naval officer, Robert E. Peary, reached the North Pole by dogsled over the ice. The South Pole was first reached by Roald Amundsen, a Norwegian, in 1911.

See also *Columbus, Christopher; exploration;* and *Magellan, Ferdinand.*

Beginning in 1603, the French explorer Samuel de Champlain explored the eastern part of Canada.

Explosive

A chemical explosive is a substance that reacts violently to produce energy in the form of heat and expanding gas. This reaction is called an explosion. In an explosion all or most of the substance reacts very rapidly and turns into gas. The heat of the explosion makes the gas expand. As the gas expands, it has enormous force. This force gives an explosion its destructive power.

The most powerful chemical explosives, such as TNT or dynamite, are called high explosives. High explosives react much faster than low explosives and explode with shattering force. High explosives are used to blast away rock and earth, and in many military weapons. Low explosives produce a slow, controlled explosion and are used in firearm cartridges, rockets, and fireworks.

Chemical explosives are very important to modern industrial society. They are very useful in large construction projects where rock and earth must be removed. They are also widely used in mining coal and other minerals.

See also *gun, nuclear energy,* and *weapon.*

The Chinese used the first explosive, black powder, in the 11th century. In the 14th century, guns and gunpower were used in the West in land and naval battles.

Extinct Animals

An animal becomes extinct when there are no more of its kind left alive on earth. In the past, animals like the dinosaurs became extinct mainly when natural conditions changed. In a different climate or without their usual food supply, the animals could not survive. Today, the actions of man present the greatest threat to animals. Man has polluted animals' homes, or habitats, with chemicals. Sometimes their homes have been destroyed completely. And man continues to hunt and kill some animals in such great numbers that they may not survive.

Laws that protect endangered animals such as the blue whale may help to keep them from becoming extinct.

Some scientists think that dinosaurs died off when the earth became cooler.

Fable

A fable is a short story that teaches a lesson about human nature. This lesson is called a moral. The author often states this moral, such as, "Look before you leap," at the end of the story. In a fable, the characters are usually animals, but they think and talk and behave like human beings.

The two most famous writers of fables were Aesop and Jean de La Fontaine. Aesop's fables were written down and collected about 300 B.C. Jean de La Fontaine was a French writer of the 17th century. He published his first book of fables in 1668 and he wrote 12 books of fables in all. He wrote his fables in verse. All of them are his versions of fables by Aesop and other writers. But La Fontaine told these stories in his own way.

Fables have long been a favorite way to tell a story for writers from many countries. Fables are still being written today. The American writer James Thurber and the English writer George Orwell have written fables that have become highly popular.

See also *Aesop*.

Fables usually have animals, such as the ant, the lion, and the tortoise, as their characters.

Fabric

Cloth for clothes and other uses is printed and dyed in huge factories called mills.

A fabric or a textile is a cloth. Fabrics are woven from different kinds of fibers or threads. Fabrics are used to make clothes, sheets, and many other useful things.

Nearly all the fabrics we wear or use are of three different kinds. One kind comes from plants. Cotton is an example. Fluffy balls of white fibers grow on cotton plants. These fibers are separated and spun into thread. The thread is then woven into cloth.

A second kind of fabric is made from the fur of animals. Wool is woven from the fleece of sheep. Like cotton fibers, wool fibers are spun into thread.

Plant and animal fibers are called natural fibers. A third kind of fabric is man-made. Nylon and polyester are made from chemicals. They are called man-made fibers. They are often cheaper than natural fabric.

See also *clothing, cotton, silk,* and *spinning and weaving.*   85

Factory

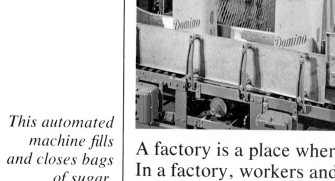

This automated machine fills and closes bags of sugar.

A factory is a place where a product is made. In a factory, workers and machines are under one roof. Materials to make a product such as toys are delivered to the factory. Workers then use machines to make, or manufacture, the toys. The toys are then shipped out of the factory to be sold.

The factory system began in England toward the end of the 18th century. Before there were factories, workers made things at home. They used their hands or small machines.

Early factories in England were dirty, uncomfortable, and dangerous places. They employed children as young as six years of age. People worked as long as 16 hours a day for very little pay. In the 19th century, authors like Charles Dickens wrote about the sufferings of factory workers. Over the years, conditions slowly improved. Today, most companies try to provide good working conditions for their workers.

See also *automation* and *Industrial Revolution*.

Fairy Tale

Fairy tales are stories of magic and romance that greatly appeal to children. Fairy tales tell about far-off lands and past times and strange happenings. They often begin with the words, "Once upon a time."

The most famous collections of fairy tales were written by European writers who used folk stories as their sources. A French writer, Charles Perrault (1628–1703), retold "Cinderella," "Sleeping Beauty," and other stories. Jakob (1785–1863) and Wilhelm (1786–1859) Grimm rewrote old German fairy tales. Hans Christian Andersen also wrote many popular tales.

See also *Andersen, Hans Christian.*

Fairy tales are often filled with strange creatures like dragons, witches, and fairies.

"Puss in Boots" (left) and "Cinderella" (right) are two highly popular fairy tales.

Family

A family is a group of people who are related to each other by birth or marriage. A person can be born into a family, such as a brother and sister. Or a person can become related through marriage, such as a brother-in-law or sister-in-law.

The most common family consists of a father and a mother and their child or children. This is called a nuclear family. In most nuclear families, the members are close to each other. Sometimes they quarrel. But they are always ready to love and care for each other.

The nuclear family can take different forms. One parent may die. Or the parents may get divorced. Then the children may be raised in a single-parent family. If a child's parents remarry, the child will have a stepmother or a stepfather. The child may also have stepbrothers and stepsisters who are the children of the stepparent.

Another kind of family is the extended family. The members of an extended family may include grandparents, aunts, uncles, and cousins. Many people have two families during their lives. The first is the family they grow up in. The second is the family they make themselves when they marry and have children.

Families live together and may even work together. Family members share many activities, such as picnics and other outings.

Farming is growing crops or raising animals on land. Usually the crops or animals are sold for food. More than 90 percent of the world's food supply comes from farms and ranches.

There are many different kinds of farmers. A farmer may grow a grain like wheat, a vegetable like tomatoes, or a fruit like apples. A farmer may raise animals like cattle or chickens. A farmer may keep bees that give honey or cows that give milk to make butter or cheese. Farming is an important industry in many countries of the world.

Agriculture is another name for farming. Scientists do research in agriculture to make farming more productive. They develop new varieties of plants and improved breeds of animals that will provide more food. They search for ways to make the soil more productive through the use of fertilizers. And they try to improve the methods farmers use to grow crops and raise animals.

See also *agriculture* and *cattle*.

Scientists have developed new varieties of wheat that provide more food from the same amount of land.

Fencing

Even when they are practicing, fencers always wear masks and protective clothing.

Fencing is the sport of fighting with swords. Fencing is a safe sport. The tip and edge of the swords are not sharp. Fencers wear a wire-mesh face mask and a jacket.

A male fencer uses one of three kinds of swords, a foil, an épée or dueling sword, or a saber. Most women fence with the foil. The foil is a thin, four-sided blade. It weighs about 17 ounces (482 g) and is about 43 inches (109 cm) long. The épée is as long as the foil but heavier. It weighs about 27 ounces (766 g). The saber has a flat blade. It is a little shorter than the foil but weighs about the same.

A good fencer must be able to move very quickly. In a match, the fencer tries to touch the opponent in order to score points. The fencer must stay on a strip which is about 46 feet (14 m) long and about 6½ feet (2 m) wide.

In major foil and épée tournaments, the swords are electrified. When a fencer touches an opponent, a bell or buzzer sounds, or a light flashes.

Fern

Ferns are plants that have been on the earth for over 300 million years. In prehistoric times, much of the earth was covered with ferns. Many were as tall as trees. Today there are several thousand kinds of ferns. They grow all over the world except in places that are covered with ice. Ferns range in size from less than an inch (2.54 cm) in height to tropical ferns that can grow to 80 feet (24 m).

Ferns have no flowers or seeds. They have tiny cells, called spores, under their leaves. Wind scatters the spores over the ground and they grow into new ferns. New fern leaves come up as tightly curled balls. As they grow, they uncurl.

Many ferns grow in damp, shady places. But some ferns will die if their roots get too much water.

Fern leaves are called fronds. They often look like large feathers.

91

Feudalism

The lord of the manor served as both ruler and judge for the people living on his lands. They, in turn, farmed his land and performed other duties for him.

Feudalism was the political and economic system in many parts of Europe during the Middle Ages. Under feudalism, a king or lord enlisted the services of another lord to become his vassal and swear loyalty to him. The vassal usually received a piece of land, called a fief, from his lord. In return, the vassal promised to fight for his lord. If the fief was large, the vassal might promise to supply the lord with a certain number of knights. To hire these knights, the vassal would grant them part of his land as their fiefs. A fief often was an estate, called a manor. The vassal became the lord of the people who lived on the land. He ruled and protected them.

During the period of feudalism, kings and lords fought each other using knights who were their vassals.

Firemen use pumping engines and long hoses to put out fires in big cities.

Fire is the light and heat given off by a chemical reaction. Three things are needed for fire: fuel, oxygen, and heat. In order to burn, the fuel must combine rapidly with oxygen. But the fuel will not burn unless its temperature reaches a certain point. A match will make a piece of paper hot enough to burn. The paper burns because its temperature is raised high enough so that it can combine with the oxygen in the air. Every fuel burns at a certain temperature called its kindling point.

Only human beings have learned how to control and use fire. Ancient peoples feared fire. They thought it was magical. Today fire is widely used by man in homes and industry.

Firemen use water to put out many fires. This cools down the material that is burning. But water will not put out an oil fire. The oil floats on the water and goes on burning. An oil fire can be put out by taking away the oxygen the oil must combine with in order to burn. A carbon dioxide fire extinguisher does this.

93

Firefly

Fireflies flash their lights to communicate with each other.

Fireflies are insects that can make their bodies "light up." They are also known as "lightning bugs." Fireflies are members of the beetle order. There are more than 1,000 kinds. They range in color from reddish brown to black. They can reach a length of one-half inch (1.3 cm). In some species, the female has no wings.

Scientists believe that fireflies produce their flashing light to attract mates. Each species of firefly flashes with a special rhythm. A firefly's light is produced by a chemical reaction in an organ on its abdomen.

Newly hatched fireflies, or larvae, are often called glow-worms. Not all species of glowworms can produce light.

First aid is help that is given before a doctor arrives to someone who has been injured or has become ill. If the accident or illness is serious, first aid can save a person's life.

One of the most important things to remember about first aid is that great care should be taken with a person who has been seriously injured or has become seriously ill. Someone untrained in first aid may do things that will cause more harm than good. The Red Cross, schools, and other organizations offer training in first aid.

The victim of a serious accident may be bleeding severely. A seriously ill person may be unconscious. An untrained person should immediately call for trained medical help. Police departments and hospitals have emergency service ambulances. At the hospital, doctors and nurses in the emergency room work quickly to treat victims of an emergency accident or illness.

See also *Red Cross*.

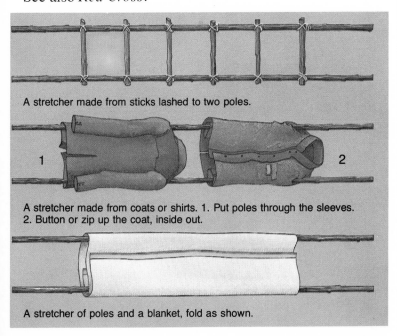

A stretcher made from sticks lashed to two poles.

1   2

A stretcher made from coats or shirts. 1. Put poles through the sleeves. 2. Button or zip up the coat, inside out.

A stretcher of poles and a blanket, fold as shown.

A stretcher made from tree limbs and clothing or blankets can be used to carry someone with a broken leg.

Fish

Fish are animals that live in the water. Most fish are cold-blooded. This means that their body temperatures are usually about the same as the temperature of the water. There are more than 20,000 kinds of fish. They live in fresh water, such as lakes and rivers, and salt water, such as seas and oceans. Some fish spend part of their lives in fresh water and part in salt water. Others stay in only one type of water. There are more fish in the world than there are amphibians, reptiles, birds, and mammals combined.

Fish swim by wriggling their bodies and moving their tails. They use their fins to stay upright, to turn, to slow down, and to stop. Fish often swim in large groups, or schools, for safety. Most fish are covered with scales that protect them like suits of armor.

Like all animals, fish must breathe oxygen. They have special breathing organs, called gills, to take oxygen out of the water. Some fish also breathe through their skin. A few

Many fish that live in the deep sea water have lights that help them attract mates.

Goldfish and other fish can be kept in aquariums. They are graceful and inexpensive pets.

kinds of fish have lungs for breathing.

Fish eat other fish and water creatures like snails and crabs. They also eat plants that live in the water. In turn, fish are eaten by other animals. People catch fish for sport and food.

During the breeding season, many fish travel long distances to mate. They lay their eggs in the water and usually leave them floating there. Out of millions of eggs, only a few survive. The other eggs are eaten by hungry fish. Most fish lay eggs but some fish, like guppies, give birth to living young.

See also specific fish.

Eels look like snakes, but they are fish.

Fishing

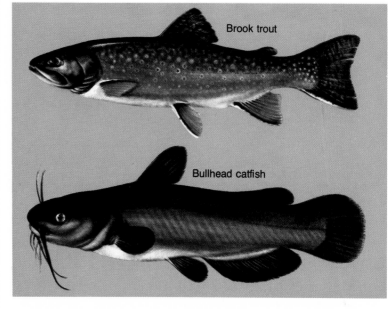

Brook trout

Bullhead catfish

Catfish and brook trout are freshwater fish that can be caught in rivers, streams, and lakes.

Fishing is the sport or business of catching fish. Commercial fishermen generally use large nets to catch fish such as tuna and mackerel.

To catch fish for fun, a beginner needs a pole, a line, a hook, and some bait. The pole can be bamboo or it can be a tree branch. One end of the line is tied to a pole. The other end is tied to a hook. For freshwater fishing, the bait can be a worm. The fisherman will feel a tug on the line when the fish bites at the bait. The fisherman then lifts the pole straight up and quickly swings the hooked fish onto the shore.

Many different kinds of fish live in fresh and salt water. A fisherman may be surprised at what he or she hooks.

Flag

A flag is a cloth sign or emblem usually flown on a pole. Most flags are rectangular or square, but some have other shapes. Countries, groups, and individuals such as the president of a country all have their own flags.

Flags first became important as a way to tell a friend from an enemy. The earliest flags were made of animal skins or other common materials. In Egypt around 4000 B.C., soldiers carried poles called standards into battle. These poles had metal birds, animals, and other objects at the end. Cloth flags were probably first used in the Orient in the 5th century B.C. The Romans also used cloth flags on their standards.

Flags became common in Europe during the Middle Ages when kings, nobles, and cities all began to fly their own flags. Flags that represented an entire country began to be used in the 16th century.

The colors and design of a flag have special meaning for a group or individual. The flag of a country may have a symbol, such as a cross or the Star of David, that is important in the country's history.

The flags of many countries are often flown at international events such as the Olympics.

Flamingo

Both the ibis and the flamingo usually gather in large flocks.

Flamingos are large wading birds that usually live in lakes and lagoons in warm areas around the world. They have long, slim legs, knobby knees, and long necks. Adult flamingos are usually red or bright pink. When flamingos eat, they put their heads upside down in shallow water and suck up tiny plants and animals.

Like flamingos, ibises live near the water. They are found in warm areas everywhere except on south Pacific islands. The ibis has a long beak that is sharply curved. Most ibises eat fish and small water animals.

Like the flamingo, the ibis is a wading bird. In fishing, it snaps its bill shut on anything live and edible.

Flatfish

"Flatfish" is a common name for many kinds of fish. There are more than 500 kinds of flatfish. They live in oceans and rivers all over the world. Flounder and sole are flatfish.

As flatfish grow, their bodies flatten out. One of their eyes moves over to join the eye on the other side of the head. Flatfish swim on the sea's bottom with their two eyes facing up.

The undersides of flatfish are white or pale. Their upper sides are usually gray. Some can change the color of their upper side to match the color of the sea's floor.

Some flatfish can change color to match the color of the sea's floor. This helps them hide from their enemies.

The flatfish changes in shape as it grows. When it's fully grown, both of its eyes are on top of its body.

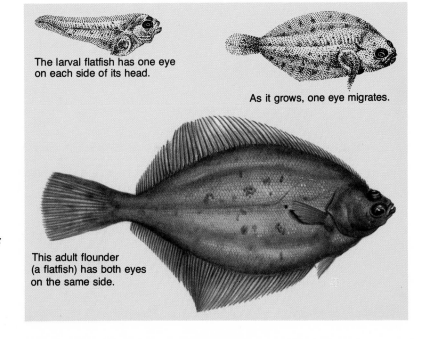

The larval flatfish has one eye on each side of its head.

As it grows, one eye migrates.

This adult flounder (a flatfish) has both eyes on the same side.

Flea

The flea is a tiny insect with a thick skin and no wings. A flea has strong hind legs that make it a champion jumper. Its body is covered with spines that help it to stick to fur and feathers.

Fleas are parasites. A parasite is an animal that gets its food by living in or on another animal. Fleas live on warm-blooded animals like dogs. Fleas suck the blood of these animals. Their bites make the animals itch.

Female fleas lay eggs that hatch into tiny wormlike larvae. The larvae crawl around eating dirt and dust. After a few weeks, they spin cocoons. Inside the cocoons, they turn into adult fleas. Fleas were once common on humans. But modern humans are cleaner than those of the past. Very few humans have fleas today.

Fleming, Alexander

Alexander Fleming (1881–1955) was a Scottish scientist who discovered penicillin, an antibotic used to treat many diseases.

Fleming graduated from medical school and then began to do research on bacteria. One day in 1928, he noticed a mold, or fungus growth, in a dish of bacteria. No bacteria were growing near the mold. He found that the mold was one called *Penicillium* and that a chemical in it killed bacteria. He named the chemical penicillin. During World War II, penicillin was used widely and saved the lives of many wounded soldiers.

Alexander Fleming shared the Nobel Prize in medicine in 1945 for his discovery of penicillin.

Penicillin is found in the mold Penicillium which is sometimes used to make cheese.

Flood

Sometimes heavy rain and melting snow will give a river more water than it can hold.

A flood occurs when large amounts of water cover land that is usually dry. The floodwater usually comes from overflowing streams, rivers, and lakes, or from high ocean tides.

Floods may occur for a number of reasons. Heavy rains, melting snow, and bad storms, such as hurricanes and typhoons, may raise the level of water in lakes, rivers, and streams. And in a storm, strong winds may cause the water to flood over coastal lands.

There are places in the world where floods occur over and over again. The Yellow River in China, the Ganges River in India, and the Danube River in Europe have flooded many times. But sometimes a flooding river can help people. The Nile River in Africa floods each year. When the water goes down again, a cover of rich soil is left on the land.

Floods can cause great damage and bring death to many people. In 1970, a flood in Bangladesh killed more than 300,000 people.

See also *disasters* and *hurricane*.

Flower

The flower is the part of a plant that makes seeds. These seeds grow into new plants. Only a few plants, including fungi, mosses, and ferns, don't produce seeds by growing flowers.

The male parts of flowers are called the stamens. They produce yellow grains called pollen. To make a seed, the pollen must reach the female part of the flower, called the pistil. The pollen fertilizes the ovules inside the pistil, and a seed is produced. Pollen may be carried from stamens to pistils by the wind, by birds, or by insects. Only pollen from the same kind of plant or from a closely related plant will make a seed.

See also *fern, moss, plant,* and *seed.*

Most flowers smell nice, but some have unpleasant odors.

The seeds of some plants grow into fruits and vegetables that people eat.

Flying

Flying is moving through the air with the help of wings or parts like wings. From early times, men saw birds and insects fly and dreamed of flying themselves. Planes fly with the help of wings and engines. Their flight is based on physical laws.

As a plane moves on the ground or through the air, the air pressure above its wings is reduced, and the air pressure below its wings is increased. This difference in air pressure produces a force called lift that pushes the wings upward. The faster a plane moves, the greater the force of lift. A plane's engines produce a force called thrust to overcome the resistance of the air to the plane.

See also *airplane, balloon, bird,* and *helicopter.*

Scientists have increased their understanding of the principles of flight by studying the shapes and movements of birds and fish.

Flying Fish

Flying fish are spineless, torpedo-shaped fish that seem to fly above the waves of the ocean. There are about 50 different kinds of flying fish. They don't actually fly. They glide in the air, using their fins as wings. A flying fish that is chased by a larger fish will vibrate its tail in the water to gain speed and then shoot out of the water. In the air it spreads out its fins and glides. Usually, the flight lasts about five to eight seconds.

Some kinds of flying fish have two sets of fins, the upper fins and the lower fins. They glide in the air using both sets. When they come down, they beat their tail fins in the water to launch themselves into the air again.

Flying fish leap to escape enemies.

Flying fish use air currents to help them glide above the waves.

Folk Art

Folk art is created by a group of people of a community, a region, or a country. Folk artists often live in rural areas. They are usually part of a group that has lived in one place for a long time and that still treasures its old traditions.

Folk artists usually do not have formal training or schooling in art. They may learn from older people in the community or they may teach themselves. Folk artists usually are skilled in a craft. They may carve wood, or make furniture, pottery, or dolls. They may do weaving or embroidery, or sew decorations on clothing.

Folk art is usually simple. Folk artists use basic designs and often repeat them. They usually try to make their art look decorative. The designs and patterns they use may have a special meaning. The designs may have religious meanings or represent nature or tell a story.

This Nigerian folk art statuette has a coat made of cowrie shells in a simple, repeated pattern.

Food

Human and all animals need food in order to stay alive and healthy. Humans have a much more varied diet than any other living thing. And unlike other living things, humans often prepare the food they eat in complicated ways. Humans eat food that may be spiced, smoked, preserved, and prepared in special ways to satisfy different tastes. Humans eat food to stay alive and to promote the body's health and growth. But humans also regard eating as one of life's pleasurable activities. For all of these reasons, the food industry is one of the largest in the world.

See also *cooking, meat, nutrition,* and *spices*.

Hamburgers became a popular food in America and are now enjoyed by people in many other countries of the world.

About two-thirds of all the people in the world work in the food industry, including farmers, ranchers, restaurant workers, and many others.

Food Chain

In a marine food chain, larger fish and marine animals eat plants and smaller fish.

Food chain is the term scientists use to describe the relationship among groups of plants and animals in providing food for each other. The illustration below shows a food chain in a pond. A single food chain seldom has more than four or five links. But in a natural environment, there will be many food chains that are connected to each other. Animals in one or more food chains will eat plants and animals in other food chains.

A food chain starts with plants. Green plants are the only living things that make their own food. All animals either eat these plants or eat other animals that eat these plants.

See also *ecology* and *plant*.

Green plants use the sun's energy and water and carbon dioxide to make their own food. This process is called photosynthesis.

A FOOD CHAIN
(1) Plants use the sun's energy to grow. (2) Tadpoles feed on the plant matter. (3) Small fish eat the tadpoles. (4) Larger fish eat the small fish. (5) A heron eats the large fish.

Football

Many people feel that football is a dangerous sport.

American football is a team sport. The two teams each have 11 players. A pointed, egg-shaped leather ball is used. The field is 100 yards (91 m) long, with two end zones of 10 yards (9.1 m) each. The team that scores the most points wins the game. A touchdown counts for six points. A touchdown is scored when one team runs or passes the ball across the other team's goal line. After a touchdown, a team can score one more point by kicking the ball over the crossbar of the goal posts. This is called a point after touchdown. A team can also kick the ball over the crossbar for a field goal at any time. This counts for three points. In Europe, soccer is called football.

Jim Thorpe, an American Indian, was an outstanding football player.

Ford, Henry

Henry Ford's first car had a gasoline engine and a steering lever instead of a steering wheel.

Henry Ford (1863–1947) was an American car maker. Ford built the Model T, the first car that large numbers of Americans could afford to buy.

Ford started the Ford Motor Company in 1903. He built cheaper cars by making all of the parts in the Ford factory, and by putting the car together on an assembly line. The first Model T, also called the "Tin Lizzie," was produced in 1908. Over 15 million were sold.

See also *automobile*.

Ford's car was cheaper and better than earlier models.

Forest

A forest is a large area of trees and woodlands. It provides food and shelter for many kinds of animals. Its trees provide wood for man. Forests also store water and prevent the erosion of the soil.

There are two main kinds of forests. One is the coniferous (co-NIF-er-ous) forest. Its trees are mainly conifer trees, such as pine, spruce, and fir. These trees are softwood trees with needlelike leaves. Conifers are mainly evergreens, which keep their leaves through the year. Coniferous forests grow in the cooler and drier areas of the world. They supply most of the lumber used for building and the wood for paper.

The other type is the deciduous forest. Deciduous (de-CID-u-ous) forests grow in areas where the weather is mild and wet. They are filled mainly with deciduous trees such as the maple, oak, and hickory. Deciduous trees are hardwood trees that lose their broad leaves each fall and grow new ones in the spring.

See also *conifer, evergreens,* and *tree.*

About 30 percent of the earth's surface is covered by forests. The Soviet Union and Brazil have the largest regions of forest in the world.

Fort

A fort, or fortification (fort-i-fi-KAY-shun), is a structure built as protection against enemy attack. The word fort comes from a Latin word that means strong. A fortification can be permanent. Or it can be made quickly and temporarily in battle, as a trench is.

The first forts came into being when people built walls to protect themselves against an enemy. Ancient cities were protected by walls and fortifications such as towers. In the Middle Ages, the castle was the most common fort. Forts began to change at the end of the 15th century when large cannons were used in war. Forts were then built with thicker walls to stop cannonballs. Some had walls made of earth and faced with stone on the outside. Early American settlers built forts called stockades. These had walls and towers, called blockhouses, that were made of logs.

In modern warfare, forts have become less important. After World War I, France built a series of forts called the Maginot Line on its border with Germany. But it was of no value in World War II.

See also *castle, Middle Ages,* and *war.*

Forts played an important part in early wars. Fort Duquesne (above), in the Ohio Valley, was the scene of one battle in the French and Indian War.

Fossil

Fossils are impressions or remains of plants and animals that once lived on earth.

Fossils were formed when plants and animals died and were covered over by sand or other loose material that hardened into rock. Sometimes only a trace or impression of the plant or animal was left in the rock, such as an impression of the leaf of a plant. Sometimes the hard parts of an animal, such as a tooth or a bone, were preserved in the rock. More often, the hard parts turned into stone themselves but kept their shape.

Some fossils are footprints of dinosaurs and other animals. Sometimes entire animals, like the woolly mammoth, have been preserved as fossils in frozen ground.

Tribolite in matrix

Fossil tree bark

Fossil ammonite

The tree bark (right) shows how living matter can harden into stone. The ammonite shell (left) and the impression of a marine animal called a trilobite (top) are fossils of animals now extinct.

Fox

Foxes generally do more good than harm. They eat small farm pests such as rats and mice.

Foxes belong to the same animal family as dogs. Foxes have pointy noses and long, bushy tails. Most foxes also have large ears for their size.

There are 12 different kinds of foxes and they are found throughout the world, even in polar regions, where the arctic fox lives. The American red fox is similar to the red fox of Europe. In America, the red fox lives on prairies and in woods. It is found from Mexico to northern Canada and Alaska. It grows to about 36 inches (91 cm) in length and has a 17-inch (43 cm) tail. The red fox usually mates with one female for life. In late winter, the female gives birth to a litter of cubs. Both parents feed and take care of the cubs until autumn, when the cubs begin to hunt for themselves. The red fox feeds on small mammals, such as mice and rabbits, birds, insects, and fruit. It also eats carrion, dead animals.

The Eiffel Tower, completed in 1889, has become a symbol of France.

France is the largest country in Western Europe and one of the oldest nations in the Western world. It has a population of 54 million people. French is the native language, and most French people belong to the Roman Catholic Church.

Modern France is a leading industrial and agricultural country in Western Europe. French wines and cheeses, as well as the French style of cooking, are enjoyed around the world. France also produces and exports cars, clothes, perfume, and textiles.

Tourism is a major industry. Paris, the capital city, is one of the world's most beautiful. Among its attractions are great art museums, including the Louvre, magnificent cathedrals like Notre Dame, fine restaurants, and sidewalk cafés. Outside of Paris, tourists enjoy French country estates called *châteaux*, vineyards, and the beaches of the Riviera.

See also *Europe*.

Photograph and Illustration Credits

All cartoons are provided by Walt Disney Productions. When more than one illustration appears on a page, credits are left to right, top to bottom.